lonely planet
kids ™

HELLO!

W9-BRN-847

PROPERTY OF

setting off from

on

in search of

with

ACKNOWLEDGEMENTS

Publishing Director   Piers Pickard
Publisher   Tim Cook
Commissioning Editor   Jen Feroze
Author   Nicola Baxter
Designer   Andy Mansfield
Print Production   Larissa Frost,
   Nigel Longuet

Published in April 2016 by Lonely Planet Publications Pty Ltd
ABN 36 005 607 983
ISBN: 978 1 76034 100 8
www.lonelyplanetkids.com
© Lonely Planet 2016

10 9 8 7 6 5 4 3 2 1

Printed in China

MIX
Paper from
responsible sources
FSC® C021741

Paper in this book is certified against the
Forest Stewardship Council™ standards.
FSC™ promotes environmentally responsible,
socially beneficial and economically viable
management of the world's forests.

Lonely Planet Offices

Australia
Level 2 and 3, 551 Swanston Street, Carlton 3053
Victoria, Australia
Phone: 03 8379 8000 Email: talk2us@lonelyplanet.com.au

USA
150 Linden St, Oakland, CA 94607
Phone: 510 250 6400 Email: info@lonelyplanet.com

United Kingdom
240 Blackfriars Road, London, SE1 8NW
Phone: 020 3771 5100 Email: go@lonelyplanet.co.uk

HOW TO USE THIS JOURNAL

1 You're off to explore our wide, wonderful world. You need a journal to make sure you never, ever forget the adventures ahead!

2 Pick up a pen and make a start by filling in your name and where you're going on the first page. Then explore your journal.

There's loads of room to record your most exciting moments, the food you eat, people you meet, places you see, and what makes you giggle, gasp or groan.

There are suggestions on the left-hand pages to help you, but you can write whatever you like. It's your journal!

! Turn to the back of your journal and watch the green rectangle as you flick toward the front. See how we did that?

The white rectangle above is just ready and waiting for your own awesome animation.

3 They say a picture's worth a thousand words and you're sure to be taking and drawing some, but there are other things that will bring memories flooding back in the future.

Hang on to tickets, leaflets, and all the bits and pieces you pick up along the way. The elastic strap will keep them safe between the pages, whether you're trekking through the jungle or exploring a city.

And even when you're home again, in these pages your trip will go on for ever.

THE LONELY PLANET EXPLORER PASSPORT

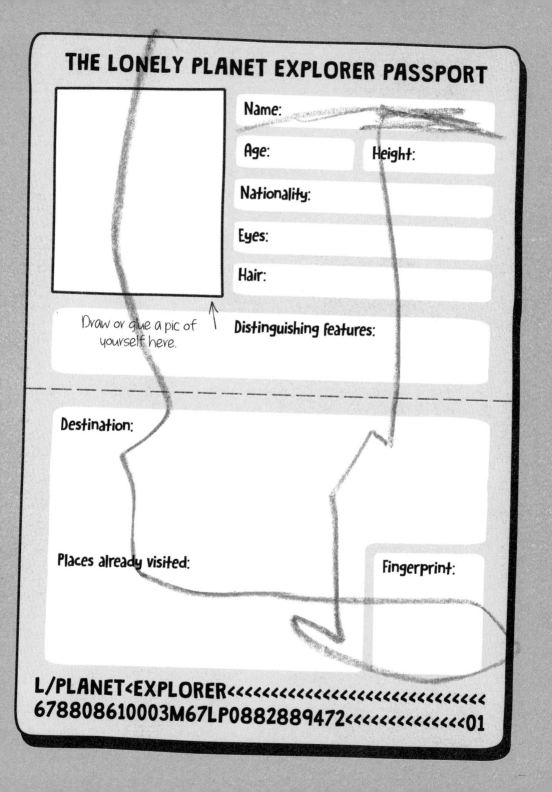

Draw or glue a pic of yourself here.

Name:

Age:

Height:

Nationality:

Eyes:

Hair:

Distinguishing features:

Destination:

Places already visited:

Fingerprint:

L/PLANET<EXPLORER<<<<<<<<<<<<<<<<<<<<<<<<<<<<<<<<
678808610003M67LP0882889472<<<<<<<<<<<<<<01

Would you like to visit the Moon? Or do you think it might lack atmosphere?

STEPPING STONES

Map out your trip by writing the main places you're visiting or those you would like to visit on these stepping stones.

Add more stepping stones yourself if you're hopping from place to place.

PACKING TRACKING

What are you bringing with you? List or draw the clothes, gadgets and other essentials in your suitcase or backpack.

How are you going to make sure your journey is fun-filled, not dullsville?

If you could travel through time, would you go forward or back?

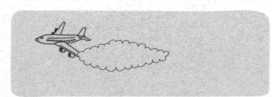

JOURNEY JOTTER

Setting out is exciting but journeys can be long. Keep a note of your outward journey highlights here.

I saw...

I heard...

the weirdest thing was...

If only I'd brought...

the funniest thing was...

Next time I'll...

EAR WORMS

Every journey has a soundtrack. Keep a note of the songs and sounds of yours.

Have you been happy today, whatever the weather?

Even if you stay at home, you will travel around the Sun each year.

WEATHER WATCH

Good or bad, the weather can be a sizzling surprise or a shivering shock. Put an X in a circle under one or more of these symbols each day. And make a note of the best and worst of the trip.

Sunny

Sunny spells

Cloudy

Rainy

Stormy

Windy

Snowy

BEST WEATHER

Where?

When?

What happened?

WORST WEATHER

Where?

When?

What happened?

DOWNTIME LIFE SAVERS

You can't be white-water rafting or whale watching every second of your trip. There are always some sitting-around-and-waiting times. Which games, books, comics, magazines, downloads and discussions are best at filling the time between adventures?

What was the first thing you saw when you opened your eyes this morning?

What do snowmen eat for breakfast?

Frosted flakes!

BEST BREAKFAST

You might stick to the same cereal at home, but on a trip meals can be seriously strange or truly delicious. Draw the best breakfast of your trip on the plate!

What did you see today that you'd like to take home with you?

MESSAGES HOME

Stuck for what to say on postcards to pals? When you have a funny idea, jot it down here in your journal for later use!

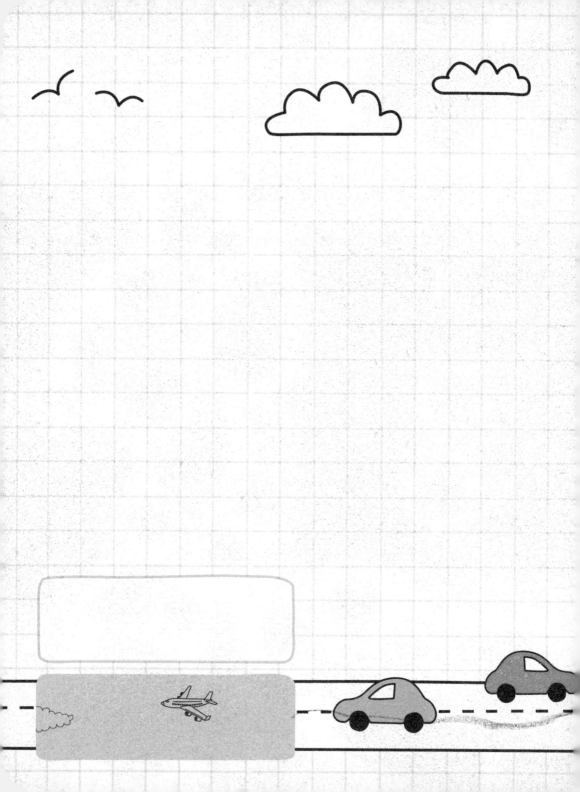

TICKET TOWERS

Gather up all the tickets from your trip and glue them into your book to make a city scene of skyscrapers.

ADMIT ONE

FLYING THE FLAG

Once you start looking for them, it's amazing how many familiar or unusual flags you'll see fluttering above you. Copy them here or invent some to celebrate your trip.

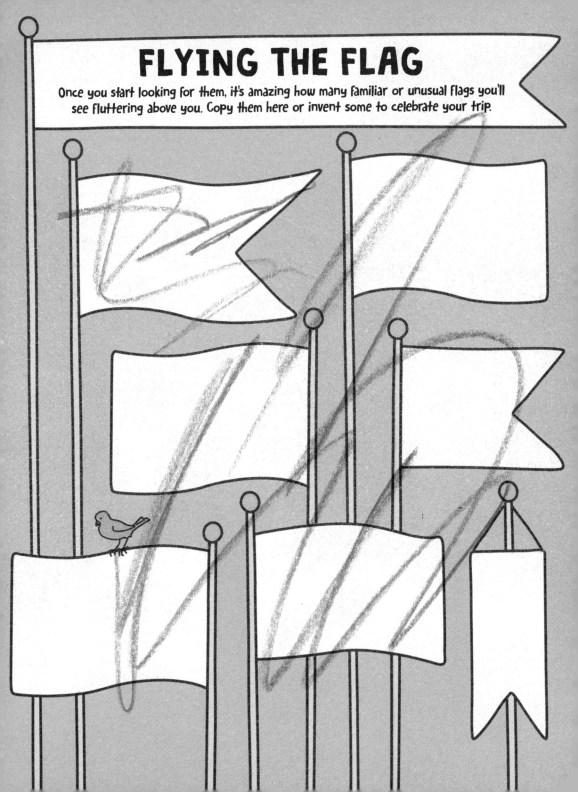

List and draw the best parts of today.

ON THE MOVE

Lying on a lounger all day? Or have you climbed a mountain, swum with dolphins, or run from a grumpy grizzly? Keep a note of the most energetic exercise you've taken this trip.

NEW FRIENDS

Sometimes you meet someone and know they'll be a friend for life. Or you spend a sunny half hour with someone you've never met before, then wave goodbye.

Write and draw reminders of the friends you meet on this trip.

Where did you go today?

SAY WHAT?

Maybe you're with someone who says the same thing over and over again. Or you learn some fun new words in a different language. Keep a record of notable quotables and catchphrases here.

ROOM WITH A VIEW

Draw what you can see from the window where you are staying or stopping to eat.

The view from:

BIGGEST FASTEST FUNNIEST

Amazing travel triumphs should be rewarded! Write in the names of those in your party who have shone in unexpected ways.

Most adventurous eater

Most cheerful

Zzzzz award for the most likely to nap

Supreme ice-cream eating champion

What are the strangest things
you've seen on a menu this trip?

_____

_____

_____

_____

_____

_____

_____

_____

_____

_____

"Waiter! What's this fly doing in
my soup?"
"Backstroke, sir."

BEST MEAL OUT

Menu

It might be a picnic in the park or a three-course feast. What did you eat for your best meal out and about? And if you really are crossing the Sahara by camel without any chance of dainty dining, this is the place to imagine the meal of your dreams.

SUPER SIGHTS

Some sights are so famous they hardly look real when you see them.
What's the most celebrated sight you've seen on this trip? Draw a picture or glue a postcard below, then write down three fantastic facts about it to impress friends back home.

THIS IS A PICTURE OF:

- WOW FACT 1:

- WOW FACT 2:

- WOW FACT 3:

List what makes you happy today.
Draw the best thing of all.

FACE IT!

It's quick and easy to draw a cartoon face. Use the templates and fill the page with the faces you see on your travels. Or draw self-portraits to show everything you feel today.

Happy

In love

Not well

Laughing

Angry

Confused

Embarrassed

LAUGH OUT LOUD

On any trip there are funny moments that shouldn't be forgotten. Jot down jokes you hear, a waiter falling into a swimming pool, a cat chasing a dog... anything that makes you grin on this trip. Add drawings or photos if you can.

HA HA

HA HA

HA HA

What do you get if you cross a wizard and a spaceship?

A flying sorcerer!

What can't you wait to tell your friends back home?

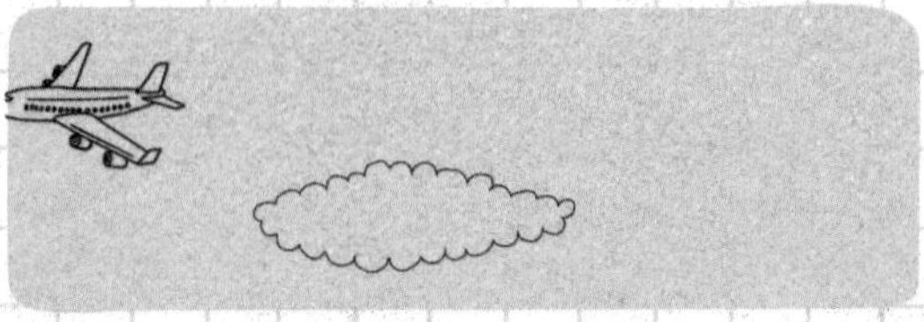

NEVER BEFORE...

Trying something new is one of the best things about travel. What will you try on this trip that you have never, ever done before? Draw or write in the circles.

What do you know now that you didn't know yesterday?

NEVER AGAIN...

What have you done on this expedition that you never, ever want to try again? Give your reasons in case you forget!

PICK OF THE POSTCARDS

Buy a couple of postcards of scenes you don't want to forget and glue them here, or add your own photos or drawings in the spaces.

Presents to take home

€

Souvenirs

£

SPENDING MONEY SECRETS

If you've got a little cash to spend on your trip, what are your plans for it?
Or has most of it already mysteriously disappeared? Make a note of what you
intend and what you spend on these pages.

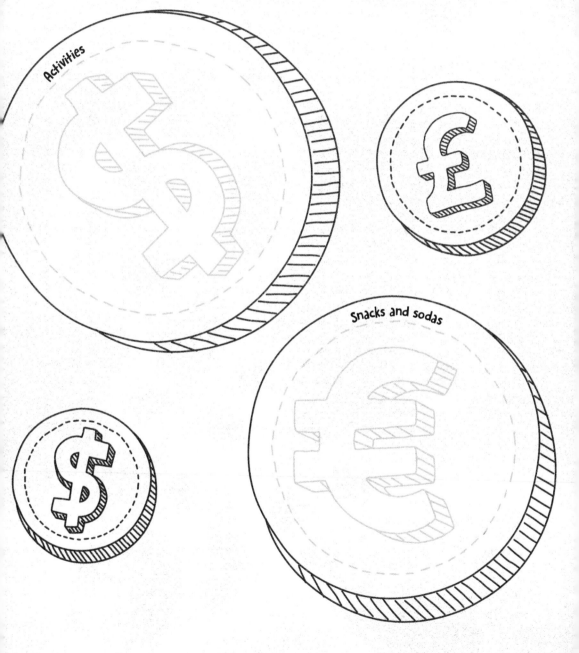

Activities

Snacks and sodas

Which country has more tourist visitors each year than any other?*

GET THE T-SHIRT

You might get the chance to buy a t-shirt to remember your trip. If not, why not design your own? What do you want to show about your amazing explorations? Design your dream tee below.

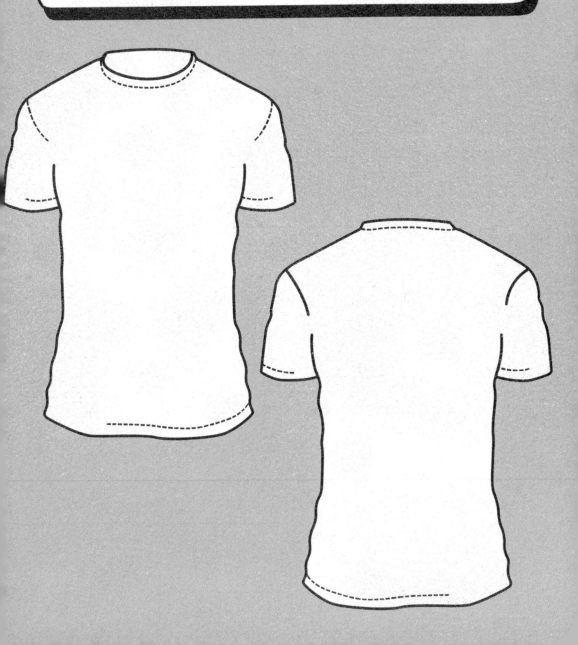

ON THE WAY WITH...

You're not alone on this expedition and by now you know all the habits of your fellow explorers. Write the good and not-so-good things about each of them. (Careful, they may be doing the same about you!)

👍 **THE CHEERS**

👎 **THE BOOS**

Draw the best thing about the trip so far in the space on this page.

FINGERPRINT FRIENDS

Dip your finger in some ink, mud, ketchup
or any other suitable substance (no, not that!)
and make fingerprints in the space below.
Then take a pen and turn them into animals,
flowers or anything else that reminds
you of this trip.

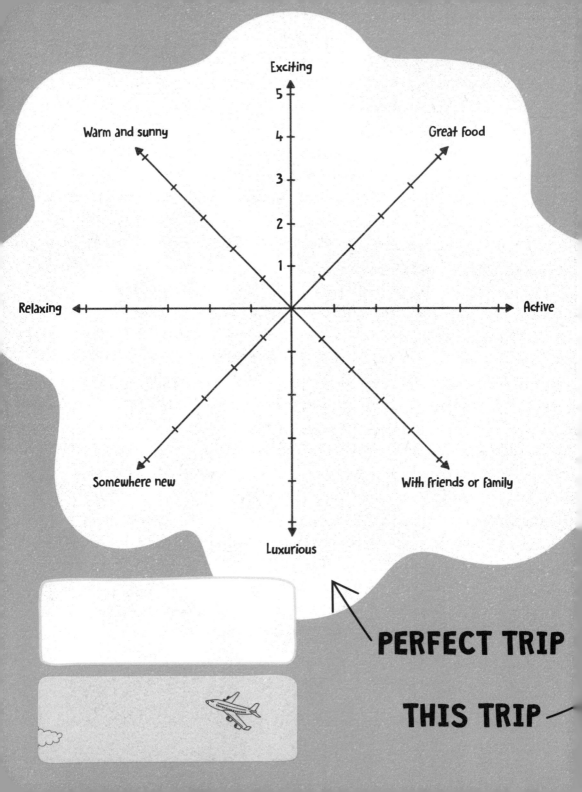

Exciting

5

4

3

2

1

Warm and sunny

Great food

Relaxing

Active

Somewhere new

With friends or family

Luxurious

PERFECT TRIP

THIS TRIP

STAR SCORES

No two explorers are the same. When you go on a trip or expedition, what's important to you? Mark each arm of the star on the left to show how you rate different parts of any trip. Connect your marks to make a shape. Then rate your present trip on the star below. How close to perfect has it been?

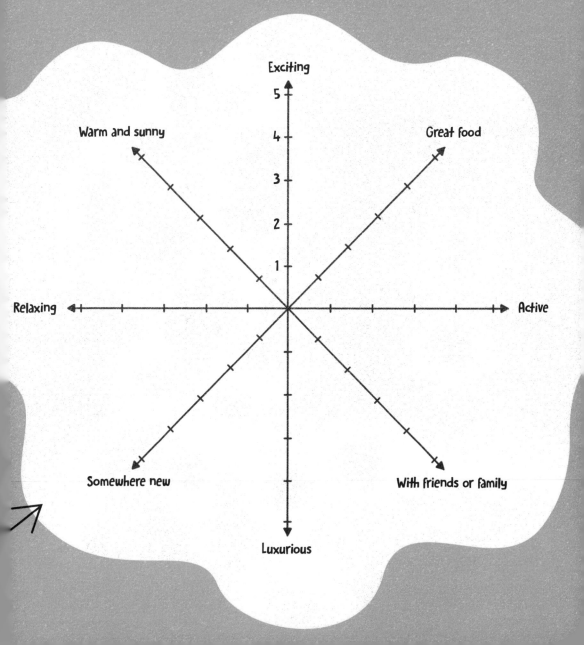

What would you say to someone thinking of making the same trip you have?

The world's travel numero uno has to be Sergei Krikalev, who has journeyed 542,921,652km (337,428,000 miles) on the International Space Station.

MEET AND GREET

On any expedition you meet lots of people along the way. You may not get to know them or make friends, but they open up a new part of the world for you. Make a note of guides, drivers, waiters, receptionists and anyone else who made a difference.

Who: What they did:

Who: What they did:

Who: What they did:

Who: What they did:

Who: What they did:

Who: What they did:

It's almost time to head for home. What do you want to do before you go?

_____

_____

_____

_____

_____

_____

_____

_____

_____

"There's no place like home!" is a famous line in which movie?*

WORD SEARCH WIZARD

Make a list of eight words below that really sum up your trip, then try to fit them into the word search grid below. Remember you can write them down, up, backward, forward and diagonally. Fill in the rest with random letters and challenge fellow explorers to solve the puzzle.

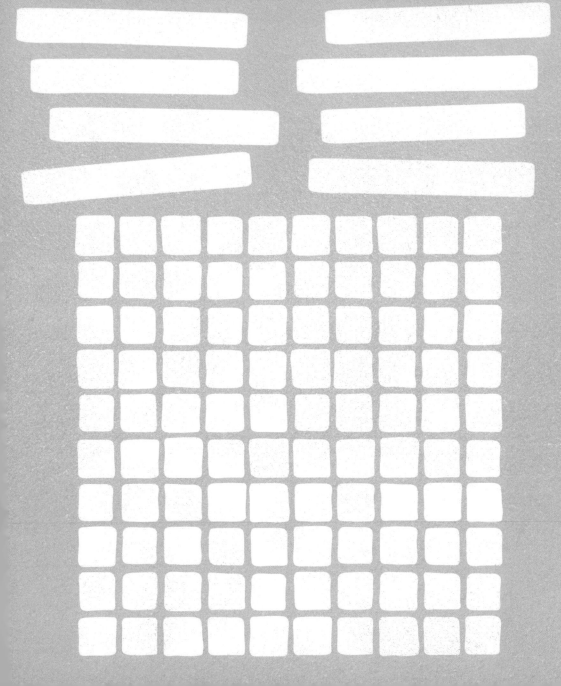

It's sad when a trip ends, but what are you most looking forward to at home?

REMEMBER YOUR ROOM

It's nearly time to go home. Maybe it feels like you've been away for ages. Do you even remember what your bedroom at home looks like? Draw it below in as much detail as you can. You'll soon be able to check out what you've forgotten while you've been exploring.

How are your fellow explorers feeling about the end of the trip?

AND FINALLY...

Write a note to your future self about how this trip has made you feel.
Promise you'll look back at your journal in five years' time
and relive every second.

THE VERDICT

What has been awesome about your trip? Write expedition high points around the stars below – the nearer the middle, the more you loved them. What will be your absolute highlight right in the middle? Food, friends, fun...or the book full of memories you're looking at right now?

BYE BYE!

Start your animation here